I0475512

Retail fashion supplier management

by

Charles Nesbitt

Copyright and ISBN page

Also by Charles Nesbitt

FUNDAMENTALS FOR SUCCESSFUL AND SUSTAINABLE FASHION BUYING AND MERCHANDISING

*

FUNDAMENTALS FOR FASHION RETAIL STRATEGY PLANNING AND IMPLEMENTATION

*

FUNDAMENTALS FOR FASHION RETAIL ARITHMETIC, ASSORTMENT PLANNING AND TRADING

*

FUNDAMENTALS OF FASHION RETAIL, TECHNOLOGY, MANUFACTURING AND SUPPLIER MANAGEMENT

*

RETAIL FASHION ARITHMETIC

*

RETAIL FASHION PROCUREMENT TEAM ROLES AND PROCESSES

*

RETAIL FASHION ASSORTMENT MERCHANDISE PLANNING AND TRADING

*

RETAIL FASHION SCENARIO AND STRATEGY PLANNING

*

THE COMPLETE JOURNAL OF FASHION RETAIL BUYING AND MERCHANDISING

Contents

PREFACE

The process of buying and selling in some form or other of goods has been with us since time immemorial. Often when one stands in bewilderment in an elegant shopping mall and wonder how all the stores are able to effectively seduce the many shoppers trawling the wide corridors to readily part with their well-earned money while at the same time enabling them to possibly enjoy a wonderful social experience.

The plan of offering goods to the potential customer is a complicated one and is a science that involves many players whose individual contributions slot seamlessly together and are so perfectly co-ordinated that it provides the perception that it is the result of one individual concerted effort.

It will be illustrated as to how the relationships of the major functions that intertwine from the conceptualisation of a product through to the presentation of a finished garment to the potential customer and in doing this demonstrates how the key areas such as buying, merchandising, technology, production, design, logistics and selling each with their unique specialised operations manage to achieve this.

The book endeavours to try and outline the basic key principles and mechanisms by which this happens and should be helpful to students, people in retailing and those who are maybe considering a career in the industry. For those who already are part of the fashion buying and merchandising community this book will be beneficial in that it provides a complete simplified overview of all the integral activities and roles that go to make up the topic and thereby will provide a broader insight into their own career.

The material of the book, other than that specifically referenced is the result of the author's own exposure to the subject during a career spanning thirty five years at a major retail organisation in Southern Africa, the support from colleagues, mentors, interaction with suppliers and own research. There has been some cross referencing to other books or technical material but the book focuses largely at a higher level on the key principles, concepts and theories and hence there is none or very little mention of retailers by name or technological packages for some key activities such as planning, allocating, critical path management, logistics and the like.

The fundamental purpose is therefore to provide the basic background that goes into the operational and technical aspects which can be universally applied. While there is merit and great benefits in the use of sophisticated technical packages that live off a common database and also integrate with one another, sadly often the prime emphasis becomes more one of mastering the system and promotes the tendency to live in a silo environment. As a result the importance tends to be focused on that single facet that the system serves rather than the broader picture. The fact that there is a relatively limited amount of material that generally describes the practice commonly known as retailing as an end to end process considering the enormous size of the industry is one of the motivating reasons for the documentation of this book.

INTRODUCTION

Retailing

Retailing is the offer of goods or services for sale by individuals or businesses to an end user. The channels by which these goods reach the final user may vary considerably and arrive via different sources such as wholesalers, trading houses or directly from the manufacturer and there are equally many differing variants in the way the goods are put on sale. Historically it is more likely that shopping would have been done at the village or town market, in a high street shop or at the "mom and pop" store which evolved over time into mass retailing stores that are often housed in shopping malls supported by smaller line shops.

More recently with the advent of the computer utilising various platforms such as the internet or social networks, shopping on line is growing exponentially using electronic payment methods with delivery via the post or with a courier man knocking on the front door of the customer bearing their purchase relatively shortly after the transaction has been processed.

The products that are put on offer will be determined by the demand to satisfy a need in the market place. Broadly the merchandise may be categorized into food stuffs, hard or durable goods such as appliances, furniture and electronics and soft goods that have a limited life span typically clothing, apparel and fabrics. Whatever the nature of the product, the key objective will be to acquire and sell the product at a price that will be more than it cost to bring it to the place of offer and thereby make a profit.

Supporting activities such as the storage, movement of the goods, technology, and marketing will endeavour to ensure that the form, function and profit objective is maximised.

In an effort to put in perspective the activities and interaction between the various functional players and their dependency and integration with each other for the end to end process of the product workflow is broadly depicted in the diagram below

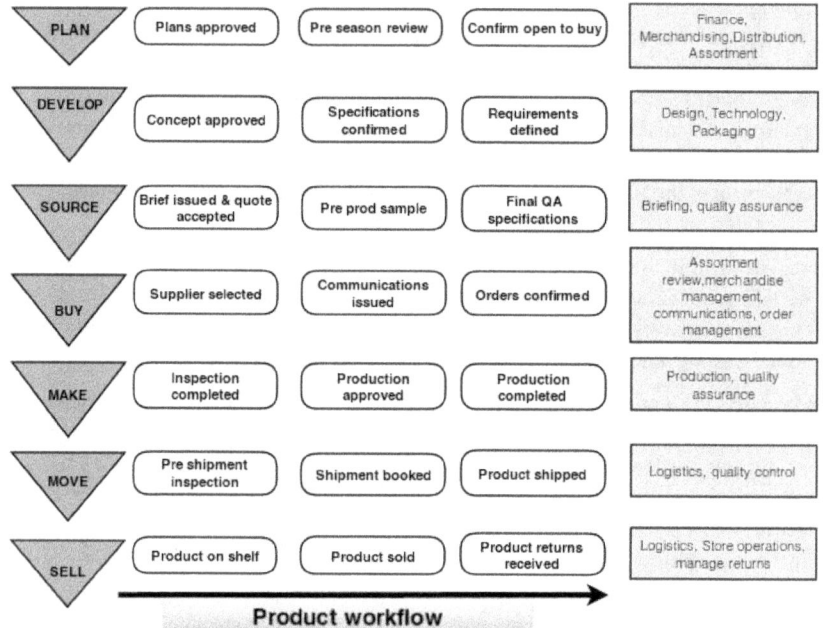

Product workflow

The distinction between supply chain and value chain should be clarified in that it is frequently misunderstood and the interpretation is varied.

Simply put, supply chain is the processes and activities that take place from conceptualisation of styles through to the procurement of raw materials and production process to the logistical operations and the eventual delivery to the end user. The value chain component is the inclusion of those functions that support the supply chain process such as the marketing philosophies. Human resource management, and consultancy resources.

The retail players

The saying "no man is an island" holds true in many spheres and this is certainly the case in the world of clothing retailing.

Various players, each with very different specialised skills are amalgamated together to deliver a completed outcome which is that of presenting product for sale to potential customers. These players are often very diverse not only in the activities that they perform but also in their personality traits which they possess. The key to a successful team is how maturely the interaction takes place and the mutual respect that every member has for each other's roles.

Below is a brief synopsis of the main player's roles and their dependency and integration with each other. The intimate details of the roles will be exposed in the future chapters as the science of retailing is explored in greater detail.

THE PROCUREMENT TEAM

The foremost players in the clothing and apparel procurement team consist typically of the following members and are described in broad terms.

Designers

Designers have a deep insight into the market they are targeting through the analysis of the changing trends and use these to provide creative direction and develop product designs for the buying teams to consider.

Usually these participants tend to think out of the box and their creative minds can challenge some of the comfort zones of other team members. What must be kept top of mind is that they need to consistently apply their intellect way ahead of time as to what they think the customer requires as opposed to their personal desires.

Typically the character traits which they will possess are that they are independent, spontaneous, extroverts, driven by ideas and are confident by nature.

Although the general perception of the word "designer" conjures up a vision of those who work at couture level, the reality is that it also includes those who are involved in creating ranges which may also be exclusive but will be more widely available and therefore can be considered as having been mass produced. Their choices will be influenced by the type of retailer they work for or the product category that they design for. The more traditional retailer which serves predominantly mature customers will be less influenced by radical fashion swings which in contrast will definitely affect the younger market's high fashion boutiques more rigorously.

Work is done at times under enormous pressure to meet critical deadlines, tough meeting schedules and involves frequent international travel. It is not surprising the perception is often one that they live a life of glory and glamour but contrary to this belief the reality is that it is not as extravagant as made out to be.

The fashion and trade shows, whether they be for yarn, fabric or garments are tiring affairs requiring hard work and stamina as is the shopping for appropriate samples, researching fashion magazines, the use of forecasting trend agencies, internet and blogs and out of all of this they need to possess the ability to then distil the emerging trends to create a storybook that will best suit their organisation's customer profiles.

The designer lives with the constant strain of knowing that their level of success will be measured by the eventual amount of money rung up at the till and getting the styling direction wrong or overextending the life of a particular look could have severe financial implications, especially in the cases where volumes are high.

The real challenge is to convince the buying teams and senior management to buy into their vision and have the confidence that what they have in mind will be commercially acceptable to the customer. The designer cannot ignore the technical aspects of the garment production as many problems can be evaded if these are taken cognisance of during the design process.

Retailers in the southern hemisphere do have the advantage that their seasons follow those of countries in the northern hemisphere which allows them to tap into the more successful designs that are trading in volume. However, with globalisation this is not always as clear cut as it was in previous years and the ability to follow as close to the season as possible requires techniques that facilitates the shortening of lead times and attempt to get the product to market as quickly as possible. The advent of communication technologies such as satellite television, internet and social media have brought exposure to different cultures, sports, films, lifestyles and trends such as those generated by specific events, health drives, environmental awareness and technology platforms that can have significant impacts on fashion which sometimes happen at very short notice.

A very important aspect is that the designer must adhere strictly to, is that of copyright. Instances have occurred that other competitor's garments are copied almost identically whether it be by style, print or design. Invariably the driving reason for this is the speed of being able to turn on a replica at a cheaper price. Although it may not be practical to register and copyright every design, any infringement can still be challenged and a consequence could occur of having the offending garments being removed from display and destroyed.

Buyers

The buyer needs to have a clear understanding of the product that is required which is in line with the trend guidelines best suited to their target customer profiles, for both the high fashion segment as well as those that best serve the more traditional customer.

It is a fact is that the role of the designer and the buyer may be a bit blurred in that they research the same fashion forecasting sites and other sources of inspiration in order to put a range of garments together. Both roles must be aware of sizing, quality and costs related to fabrics, trimmings and production. To achieve this successfully they must be flexible enough to develop and buy the most suitable product that is in line with the prescribed strategy and achieves the desired profit margin in keeping with the set down targets. The evaluation of competitive activity and product ranges through regular store visits and comparative shopping provides the knowledge required to keep ahead of the field.

Effective communication and presentation skills are a prerequisite to brief and interact with suppliers as well as presenting product reviews to colleagues within their own group at all levels of seniority. With this comes the need to be able to accept criticism and resolve problems in a mature manner. The sad fact is that frequently when the analysis of the success of the range is evaluated at the end of the season, if the results are disappointing it is not uncommon for the buyer to shoulder the emotional burden of the poor performance. The truth of the matter is that the range was presented on more than one occasion to all team players including senior management all of whom signed the range off but in the final analysis they are more often than not, as is human nature, reluctant to be accept any proper accountability.

Coupled to ability to understand the wants of the customer is the sourcing of the most suitable supplier that will be selected for the specified product types in terms of their particular skills, technical ability, costing efficiency, attitude, transparency, honesty, focus on quality, communications and competitiveness while still meeting the ethical criteria that are acceptable to society.

A large part of the task will be to maintain good relations with suppliers, while at the same time being able to assertively negotiate prices with them and make sure the planned stocks are delivered on time. Communications need to be clear and specific to avoid disputes over issues which may arise through vague and confusing messages. For these reasons they need to be confident, take decisions based on results and be driven by a sense of urgency.

The buyer has to be multi-talented in that as well as being creative they also need to monitor the sales objectively and be flexible enough to react accordingly in terms of turning on or turning off production and transferring fabric and components to more appealing product styles where sales performance and fast emerging trends dictate.

What is key to be a successful buyer is the ability to work as part of the overall team and influence the rest of the team's activities which could be in the form of a managerial and developmental capacity that could also include both their peers and superiors.

The display of emotional maturity and commercial acumen within the controlled parameters as set by the merchandising arm in terms of the budgets, the number of product options and display space constraints is absolutely essential.

The same principle applies to the relationships that need to be maintained with the technical teams in regard to the use of the most appropriate fabrics which meet the product form and function demands in addition to ensuring that the brand standards of the garment are observed.

The fact that potentially the buyer together with the other retail players will be dealing with three to four seasons simultaneously at different stages for each season makes their task even more complicated. To clarify the phenomenon a bit further, the journey of this book attempts to describe the process from beginning to end for one season but while trading in the current season the thoughts and strategies are being developed and documented for two or possibly three seasons ahead followed by the range development leading up to the production taking place for next upcoming season.

The ability to absorb and interpret vast amounts of information from various sources, much of which originates from complex IT systems, can present a challenge to those who are not analytically minded. Systems have altered the scope of the traditional buyer from being a pure "touchy feely art skill" to having to develop basic technical abilities through the continual emergence of innovative systems which have become a great advantage to the role.

Some buyer's, such as those for knitwear, ladies structured underwear, tailoring and footwear will require more expert fabric and garment construction knowledge of their respective industries in comparison to individuals who select the more straightforward cut, make and trim products such as dresses, blouses and casual trousers.

As the trade environment has become more global and through information technology development it is much faster, interactive and has enabled business to be done more effortlessly from a home base interacting with many different countries. A great deal of the job is done amongst many new emerging countries which has led to a need for urgency and nimbleness in order to locate the most effective plants that meet the quality requirements, be able to assess the required technical abilities, understand the economic and cultural demands of the respective countries as well as the logistical peculiarities and government regulations that may exist.

The sourcing of production has to take on different approaches as the pros and cons of dealing internationally needs to be carefully weighed up against those of dealing with the ever diminishing number of local suppliers. A critical factor is that suppliers must be ethical in terms of labour practices, remuneration, waste management, working conditions and safety. If such conditions are not met it is counter to the interests of the retailer to be associated with such suppliers from both a moral point of view and the exposure of malpractices could lead to negative media reports and the retailer will suffer the consequences that accompany such deeds. The measurement of performance is therefore key to gauging the effectiveness of suppliers.

In larger organisations a buyer will probably be supported by an assistant or trainee buyer who will normally be a person who wishes to pursue a career in the field. They will be largely responsible for the organisation of the ranges, perform some clerical work whilst preparing products for garment reviews, monitoring the product development critical path and production milestones, liaising with suppliers and technology as well as deputising for the buyer when they are out of the office.

A point to note is that the relationship between buyers and suppliers often develops into more than a pure business association due to the fact that they spend much time travelling together and working closely with one another building ranges. Close familiar relationships frequently make it difficult to maintain a business like association for the mutual benefit of both parties and can cloud business decision making and judgment. The temptation of bribery and incentives in exchange for placing large orders may be desirous. For newer naïve buyers the rule that the supplier is not your friend should be firmly applied simply because they are more easily seduced by grandiose lunches and gifts as many have unfortunately found out the hard way when they move on and are no longer of great importance to the particular supplier.

A way of balancing the workloads or ranking of buyers and merchandisers is to evaluate the actual number of suppliers, stock keeping units or barcodes being handled by each buyer and then make comparisons regarding workload and productivity of each buyer to established benchmarks.

Merchandisers

There is a novelty t-shirt on the market which has the following statement blazon across the front panel which reads as follows – *"Merchandise Planner – we do precision guesswork based on unreliable data by those of questionable knowledge"*. Although the humour can be appreciated it should be known that this statement is not too far from the truth as the success of merchandising objectives is reliant on many diverse inputs.

The merchandiser or planner applies their focus on maximising profitability from the business end. This is done largely through the analysis of historical sales and the influence of the trend direction to determine the range categories and product breakdown within the overall sales budget.

The role defines what stock levels are required to meet the preset targets such as seasonal stock turnover or forward stock covers based on the sales trends over time. Knowing these requirements, the merchandiser will determine what intake or purchase quantities are needed at any point in time in the season for the total department and each product category.

The level of the budgets will determine the quantity of options in relation to styling, colour palette, size spans, pricing structure and levels of quality per category that will best service the customer for the time that the goods are expected be on offer prior to a new variety of product being introduced in line with the strategic predetermined seasonal themes.

The merchandiser's job has to be to provide guidance to the buyer to procure within the budget parameters. In short it can be described as providing the buyer with a shopping list or range plan that allows them to go out and fill in the blanks on the plan while buying product. This activity requires the careful management of the "open to buy" which can often be a source of tension between the buyer who always tends to want more and the merchandiser who holds the purse strings. A good deal of emotional maturity and teamwork on both sides is therefore critical for a successful partnership.

Sadly the merchandising role is often branded as a dull, boring number crunching task in accordance with mathematical calculations and while it is this, it can be better described as a creative manipulation of numbers. This task is highly rewarding when positive trade results are achieved or alternatively equally as depressing when these do not materialise. The role can be likened to that of a husband who places his entire salary on a dead cert horse at the races which was by no means appreciated by his wife. However when the horse won he was similarly unpopular for not putting more money on the horse!

Like the buying role, the merchandiser deals with different activities simultaneously as part of the team across a number of seasons and therefore requires high levels of multi-tasking and re-prioritising in the forward planning, problem resolution, critical milestone management, analysis and timeous action implementation.

As the actual trade takes place the results need to be carefully analysed and immediate action plans initiated in order to maximise the opportunities and minimise the levels of markdowns that erode the profits. For these reasons they need to be logical, reliable, and consistent in order to take decisions based on fact.

The regular timeous generation of reports detailing sales analysis, stock levels and forward planning needs are distributed to all team members and to senior management. Often numeric information and commercial analysis is demanded on an immediate ad-hoc basis which adds pressure to the job function and can be very disruptive to routines which in such situations requires the merchandiser to adapt quickly and effectively.

The merchandiser plays an integral role during the presentation at product reviews from the numbers perspective which influences the agreed product mix and justification of the levels of sales budgets.

A detailed understanding is necessary of the stores and the customer profile inherent to respective stores that are best met through the attributes of the ranges in terms of styling, colour and size that are put on offer within the store space constraints. The task is best described by the saying "plan each store as if it is your own" which could never be truer.

With sophisticated IT development and the availability of various software packages, some of which may be developed exclusively for the retailer, will provide quick sales analysis, production planning and afford the ability to make sound decisions based on accurate data. This information is especially necessary to give guidance to the allocator or distributor who will be sending the appropriate quantities to satisfy the store's needs as well as give direction as to the level of repeat buys for products that are trading above expectations.

Some organisational structures do differentiate the allocation function between the merchandiser who focuses on the forecasting and production planning and that of the allocator or location planner who will be responsible to distribute the product to the stores in the most appropriate combinations of styles, colour and sizes that meet the store profiles. This function can be housed as an extension within the buying division or may be part of a separate centralised group where an allocator may be responsible for a diverse number of departments. The benefits of such a centralised structure is that there could be a cost saving advantage especially where smaller departments do not warrant a dedicated staff member but added to this is a pool of knowledge which develops a highly skilled team who are able to cross pollinate information, coordinate inter departmental promotions effectively and develop consistent techniques and skills. The identification of common emerging trends will contribute to the optimisation of sales and assist in the control of stock quantities at a very detailed level and thereby maximise profits. Close connections to the departmental merchandisers is maintained to ensure that their actions are aligned to the departmental strategy and plans.

The need for the diversification of the function also makes more sense from the point of view in that where the distribution function is retained within the department it inevitably adds to the increasing workload of the merchandiser. The departmental merchandiser task has more and more been impacted on by the development, the implementation and mastering of complex and sophisticated information systems that analyse sales and stock with added forward planning functionalities.

Many such systems are able to integrate with other supporting IT platforms such as supplier performance, technological measurement, critical path management, ordering, logistical and store systems. The added management of a complex allocation system that is necessary to move the stock to stores is more and more difficult with the result that the incumbent is in danger of being drawn into concentrating on and coping with the intricate detail. As a result, the merchandiser runs the risk of losing sight of the bigger objectives as set out in the strategy and operational plans and the consequent degrading of the inherent merchant intuition becomes very real.

The merchandiser needs to effectively manage and develop the merchandising team which can, not unlike the buying role, consist of an assistant merchandiser or trainee who aspire to be a merchandiser.

The role ensures cohesion of activities that have to be synchronized based on actual sales performance through the formalised interaction with other stakeholders such as the buyers and technologists. This contact is usually in the form of regular, typically weekly, departmental meetings where corrective decisions and plans of action are agreed. Frequent association with the points of sale in stores through written communications and reports as well as formal site visits are critical to keep aligned with the customer's preferences and emerging trends and confirm that the stores are sharing the same vision of the overall strategy.

The need to guide suppliers assertively in terms of prioritisation and the achievement of deadlines is critical to meet the suitable stock requirements at any point in time, particularly in relation to peak seasonal periods or key events. For example, once winter breaks, which it does every year except the exact date is not easy to predict, the objective is to have the right stocks in place such as knitwear, thermal underwear, scarves and the like in sufficient quantities to meet the rush. The usual manner to assist in the anticipation of the weather trend is done through reference to previous years data when the weather changes happened which also help to understand variations in out of ordinary performance at particular times. The challenge is therefore to have the appropriate quantities in the stores at the vital time while the maintenance of the balance of stocks must be adequate to cater for the demand without overstocking the stores ahead of planned stock targets. Events such as Easter, Christmas, Valentine's Day and Mother's day are easier to predict and the right levels of stock can be made more accurately available at the right time.

Where suppliers do not meet the required delivery dates, the merchandiser needs to manage the consequences that have to be applied for the underperformance. This can result in some very sensitive and emotional discussions and the negotiation of penalties typically in the form of discounts, sale or return agreements or even total cancellation which will no doubt impact negatively on both parties.

Technology
Technical Teams consist broadly of the fabric and garment technologists. Fabric technologists are highly trained specialists who focus on typically woven or knitted disciplines. Specialised products such as knitwear, tailoring and footwear require added knowledge of components and specific production machinery.

A major portion of the fabric technologist's task is the development and innovation of new fabrics and the enhancement of existing products. New fibres and blends of fibres such as the blending of natural and synthetic fibres, addition of chemicals to finishing process will possibly lead to new inventions and improvements such as better washability, softer handles, easy care properties like easy to iron, crease resistant finishes, rot resistant applications, seamless or seams that are glued that allow for smoother looks particularly for under garments, the evolvement of elastane products such as lycra which revolutionised active and casual wear and the enhancement of thermal properties of winter undergarments. The success of such developments which add to the profitability as well as the form and function necessitates a close working relationship with suppliers, mills and value adders.

Garment technology have the responsibility to ensure that the make-up of the garment meets the set down criteria and the componentry like buttons, interlinings and threads are of the standard that is functional and are not inferior.

Many factories have developed specified technological capabilities that have been built around the production of a particular category of garments relevant to them which vary from factory to factory or even within the same plant. The garment technologist must understand this implicitly and exploit this knowledge to its fullest.

The relationship with the commercial team is sometimes strained as the ideal level of form and function can be challenged by the need to market the product at the most commercially competitive price.

The objective of the garment technologist is to ensure that quality is not compromised. The tasks essential to achieve this can be varied, for example, the assessment of potential manufacturers and fabric mills to ensure that the established standards are achievable, the specification of raw materials, overseeing sampling stages and ensuring that any delays which may result through the process do not compromise the delivery prerequisites.

In safeguarding that the all quality standards are met particularly through the inspection of garments, inspectors need to possess specific skills. Quality controllers should be ethical, sincere and honest, open mindedly being willing to consider alternatives, be diplomatic and tactful in their dealings with people and are able to actively observe their surroundings as well as perceive and adapt to varying situations.

The technologist has an intimate knowledge of the supplier base through historical awareness as well as from continually researching new and existing suppliers. As the sourcing specialist they have to guide buying teams in the selection of the most appropriate manufacturer for the various types of product. It is also very essential that they are conscious of the fabric prominence for the forthcoming season as dictated by the strategies and budget levels to ensure that there is sufficient capacities at the relevant mills to meet the overall demands without compromising quality.

The task of assessing potentially new suppliers is a role that may be included in the stable of the technical team or it may be hived off to defined sourcing specialists who are knowledgeable team members that recognise the strengths and weaknesses of suppliers and based on this where best to place orders accordingly.

Suppliers are assessed on various criteria such as their management infrastructure, financial stability, specialised equipment availability, fabric specialty, levels of innovation, fashion or basic production orientation, the other retailers they serve, their flexibility of cost negotiability and social responsibility policies. Other external factors that may well influence the selection of suppliers could be those like prevailing exchange rates, remuneration policies and physical locality.

In summary, the significance must be emphasised that the diverse buying teams all have to have a clear informed understanding of each other's roles and priorities and that they are aligned to ensure all their tasks are integrated to achieve the goal of delivering consistent quality products manufactured by appropriately skilled suppliers on time all the time. This is especially imperative in the case of more complex products such as corsetry, tailored garments and knitwear.

The handling, packaging, storage and movement of the product through the supply channels has to be done in such a way that the quality of the product is not allowed to deteriorate in any way whatsoever. As some product is sourced from more distant locations a newer trend is to contract the technical function out to approved independent technical service providers or to trusted garment and fabric suppliers themselves who understand and are committed to the standards required. These service providers are thereby able to approve samples, perform quality control and be responsible for the eventual release of the finished product.

SUPPLIERS

Sourcing suppliers
The assessment of a prospective supplier or vendor, mill, dye house, fibre producer, processor, trimming and component contractor, packaging supplier and printer is a process that needs to be done thoroughly in order to ensure that they meet all the required criteria to manufacture the product in mind.

In principle there are four different methodologies of purchasing product.

The majority of garment purchases conducted by the retailer is as per the processes described in this book which is conceived based on inputs from the design, buying, merchandising and technical teams whereby the criteria of fabric, components, style and manufacturing as well as the packaging are dictated to the supplier.

Secondly, as is practiced by the more traditional retailers is where they buy their own fabric and allocate it out to a cut, make and trim supplier. The supplier may or may not offer a style, which could be provided by the retailer to a number of different suppliers to obtain a quote for the manufacture of the product according to a labour minute rating. The price of the fabric is static as it is supplied by the retailer. The downside of this methodology is that the retailer must have a technical understanding of fabrics which means that the buying team needs to be more knowledgeable and have added skills which are not always readily available in the labour market. There is also the need to invest in fabric stocks and have a detailed understanding of minute rates or manufacturing costs of the supplier. On the plus side of cut, make and trim manufacturing is that it enables the ability to cost accurately, be more flexible in selection of styling and achieve a greater speed to market.

A third methodology of sourcing is the direct purchase of a completed ready designed garment from the supplier where the retailer's brand label is inserted and the style is procured exclusively for the retailer.

Lastly there is the option to procure popular brands directly out of the supplier's range. In this case it is likely that there will be no flexibility in terms of modifying the style and often the investment of building a store within a store concept may be required. Pricing tends to be at a premium and commonly minimum order quantities apply.

The researching of new, cheaper, innovative and exciting sources of supply in order to maintain a competitive advantage in the market place is an ongoing process, as is the need to maintain a sustainable relationship with current core suppliers which comes with a continual effort to improve their delivery standards of product. Suppliers are expected to be consistently reliable, effective and efficient to retain the business of their clients as the success of the retailers is the guarantee of continued acceptance of the product that they produce.

A constant balance of those products which are sourced from local suppliers and that which are manufactured off shore is important. As off shore suppliers improve in terms of quality, equipment and workforce living standards there is an increasing pressure on costs and therefore the sources do not remain geographically static.

Fashion buying was originally focused in the Far East in Hong Kong and Taiwan but costs are increasing faster than they have in the past as well as pressure is being placed on authorities to elevate minimum wage bands. It is therefore not surprising that production is moving to more cost efficient areas such as Indonesia, Bangladesh, Pakistan, Cambodia, and Vietnam while production in Madagascar and Mauritius has also become prevalent.

Hong Kong and Taiwan have now become more the management and design centres who procure from alternative production plants. The ease of increased technology, the relaxing of bureaucratic barriers as well as cheaper travel has enabled the transfer of production to be relatively easy and flexible. Migration of production to newer countries brings limitations and therefore it is important to maximise efficiencies in the current countries where goods are produced while at the same time sourcing alternative manufacturing plants that will meet the ethical and quality standards of the retailer.

Added to this is the probability that the larger the offshore supplier is, the more the likelihood is that the retailer will be less important in their lives and if need be, the order can be more easily forfeited. The converse is that if the overseas supplier is small the possibility exists that the production may be outsourced to other vendors who the retailer may not even know about. Overseas factories seldom readily have excess production capacity and that this together with the longer transport lead times make the possibility of repeat orders within the same season improbable.

Sourcing internationally does, at face value, often appear to be very attractive but there are factors that need to be taken into account which can lead to additional unforeseen costs as well as logistical challenges particularly in terms of lead times. The re-organisation of production can therefore be perplexing and the savings that may be apparent up front could indeed be decimated later down the line.

Keeping track of the off shore supply chain at times presents some complex challenges and makes it very difficult to monitor the progress of product at all times. An extreme illustration of such a scenario is where the process commences with the raw material producer who passes the product onto the commodities traders whose purchasing agents sells them onto the garment manufacturers. In the procedure local distributors could be involved to deliver the raw materials to the garment manufacturing plant. Secondary vendors for outsourced processes are frequently utilised before the product is delivered eventually to the local exporters and freighters administered by agents on behalf of the larger trading houses who are the frontline liaison with the retailer.

Advantages may be enjoyed by having a dedicated foreign office in key cities to control the management of suppliers and product. Obviously this does come at an added cost and should only be considered when a critical mass in that foreign country is achieved. However, the formation of such an organisation must be assessed on merit as to whether it is viable or not. Typically such a team will consist of two or three merchandisers, possibly buying and sourcing specialists together with maybe three or four quality controllers who spend two to three days a week in the factories focusing exclusively on the retailer's orders. The foreign office owns the relationship with the supplier and are able to exert pressure to ensure critical deadlines are met. Communication is easier and faster as such teams are self-managed and can be flexible in evaluating priorities.

The extreme example of the complexity of dealing with offshore suppliers is that of the world's largest trading house being the Hong Kong based sourcing and logistical company, Li Fung. They own no factories or mills but simply play matchmaker between poor countries factories and vendors which have favourable labour rates and costs and the global retailers for whom Li Fung handle the logistics.

Li Fung represent some fifteen thousand suppliers across sixty countries which enable them to procure very high volumes and have them produced in a fraction of a time that a single supplier would take to complete. It is not surprising that consequently they are known as the "Walmart of purchasing" and the sheer size of the organisation makes it difficult to pin point the true sources of the product and they have been alleged from time to time to be linked to several calamities in some dubious factories.

Where the retailer is dominant in their target market and the volumes are substantial enough it is advantageous for them to cut out the middleman agent and procure directly from the source. By doing this an advantage is gained over their competitors and they do not end up subsidising the supply chain for their rivals especially where full containers are bought on a repeat basis. Advantage is also to be gained through using a buying agent or consolidator to combine the products into full container loads where they purchase from multiple off shore suppliers.

Currency exchange rate fluctuations may well change the advantage of buying off shore, as will quota limitations which could change in the exporting country due to the fact that costs will probably increase should the availability of the quotas become scarcer.

The management of offshore deliveries is more complex and if minimum order quantities are imposed they can lead to higher storage costs and inventory investment together with varying transport charges.

The intricate nature of international freight forwarding requires either an in house dedicated team or the need to outsource this function to an agency to take on the responsibility.

Often the additional travelling and increased management costs are not taken into account when considering product quotations. The opening of foreign offices with sourcing, quality control and buying teams in itself can be a considerable additional overhead that needs to be established, staffed and equipped and is excluded from the base garment cost.

Frequently the bulk offshore deliveries have to be unpacked and repacked and labelled after allocation that results in multiple handling which adds considerable cost and time delay.

For the reasons above the viability of sourcing from foreign suppliers has to be carefully considered in terms of the minimum volumes that need to be procured to achieve the benefits while at the same time being able to exceed the sales potential without putting strain on the warehouse storage capabilities.

It is therefore strategically beneficial if the supply chain from overseas is as short as possible with the minimum of cross over proprietorship points, for example, the allocation of product while it is in transit lessens the pressure of receiving and warehousing of the goods before being withdrawn for picking and packing. The possibility exists that the goods can bypass the storage stage and be delivered directly to the pick pack areas of the distribution centre. This type of approach might be appropriate for one off promotions and special events.

The advantages of a local supplier base is quicker potential delivery to market, more flexible production with easily manageable inventory quantities and less complicated administration, quality control and payment methodologies. For local suppliers the trend has also shifted towards smaller production infrastructures with specialisation on exclusivity and individualistic styling.

The relationship between retailers and local suppliers is most often one of mutual interdependence all of which has to be weighed up against the cost and innovation advantages of off shore suppliers. The manufacture of replenishment core type product is better suited to local manufacturers as it calls for the fine-tuning of styles, colour and size ratios which are easier to adjust. There may also be pressure from the authorities to encourage local production through the various "Buy Local" promotions in order to stimulate the local industry and satisfy the employment initiatives in the political arena.

It stands to reason that the less suppliers there are, the less the burden of supplier management will be with regard to different administration models, quality control and varying costs.

A strategy to rationalise suppliers eliminates smaller, incompatible, problematic suppliers who are often more demanding in terms of the time required to manage them compared to the effort spent on more substantial, streamlined producers and enable effective performance management.

The larger the quantities allocated to fewer suppliers will lead to lower cost prices through the economies of scale advantage as well as the benefit of the delivery of improved quality and reliability. Management communication and the mutual interdependence with specialised service provision will undoubtedly lead to a competitive advantage.

There are however risks involved in dealing with too few suppliers in that the exposure to greater innovation is limited and complacent suppliers tend to offer more and more of the same or wait for the retailer to provide ideas and designs. Often the production methods are inflexible which could result in a relationship of mistrust and frustration.

Newer suppliers can be added to the core base of suppliers, however, the number of suppliers in total should remain constant through the consistent measurement of performance including formal review processes being in place for existing suppliers. If they do not meet the performance criteria they run the risk of elimination.

The performance review and assessment of suppliers should not be done in isolation by each department that they supply but preferably conducted across the business as a whole which will deliver more objective and consistent results and thereby will avoid mixed messages being given to suppliers.

Other pitfalls that retailers need to be aware of is the differing perceptions of the suppliers versus that of the buyers. Typically buyers view suppliers as being frequently older and more experienced, full of excuses and promise the world. From the suppliers point of view the buyers are young and inexperienced, abuse their buying power and utilise threats to make unrealistic demands and apart from being busy all the time, the formation of a sustainable relationship is disrupted due to the regular changing of staffing in departments.

It is not uncommon that buyers and designers tend to make last minute changes to designs, trims, quantities and colours which puts immense pressure on suppliers and consequently leads to the need to work excessive overtime hours or over book production capacity. As a result they may end up using unqualified outside vendors in an effort to accommodate the revised unreasonable deadlines and can thereby easily transgress the compliance criteria.

Conscious efforts are essential to influence the relationship to be one of joint co-operation and respect, the conducting of informed cost price negotiations with better transparency with regard to each other's needs and the working together to achieve solutions that will be for their mutual benefit.

There are some key questions that need to be answered before embarking on a relationship with a potential supplier which are:

What are the supplier's capabilities and specific skills?

Do they have design facilities and what level of innovation is evident?

Do they have the capacity requirements to meet the required volumes?

Is the planning of production stable in that it minimises changeovers and keeps labour fully utilised so that orders are not shifted around dependent on which customer is shouting the loudest.

Are they financially stable? Do they meet the criteria that ensures payment to their raw material suppliers being secure and guaranteed?

Do they have the appropriate equipment to deliver the envisioned product?

Is the production sub contracted to other vendors and do these producers also meet the same required compliance standards?

What are the initial costing indications in comparison to alternative sources?

Which other major retailers do they supply?

What management and liaison structures are in place?

What are their quality standards like and do they have current valid compliance audits from an accredited recognised test house?

Do they have the ability to produce or source in smaller batches to maximise flexibility and speed?

How close are they to their component suppliers?

Where are they located and will that have any bearing on meeting the delivery lead times, delivery demand schedules and costs?

Do they have any long term strategic expansion plans?

Does the physical building structure meet all building specifications, safety requirements and provide the appropriate facilities to accommodate a production environment?

Is there evidence that they are ethically compliant in terms of staff hours of work, remuneration policies and adherence to accepted norms of terms of employment?

Do they meet the environmental requirements in terms of health and safety of the workers?

Do they utilise any banned substances in the production process and what is the policy for the safe disposal of waste effluent?

Are the raw material suppliers reputable and certified?

What are their laboratory facilities or which testing facilities do they use?

The format of these initial audits can be formalized in a matrix form and scorecard values can be weighted according to the level of importance that can be depicted through a relative score compared to other suppliers which ensures a more objective assessment and structured plans of action for suppler selection.

A simple example of such a supplier rating matrix is as follows

	QUALITY	CAPACITY	GROWTH	COSTING	ENVIRON-MENT	SOCIAL	INNO-VATION	LIAISON	TOT	WEIGHTED AVERAGE
WEIGHTED IMPORTANCE	6	6	5	7	5	5	5	6		
SUPPLIER A	20	15	25	30	15	15	10	20	150	108
SUPPLIER B	25	20	30	25	20	20	25	10	175	123
SUPPLIER C	30	30	10	25	20	20	30	20	185	132

Key areas of compliance focus in the drafting of an audit report

Social compliance refers in the main as to how the company treats its employees and their perspective on social responsibility. The point of reference is to a minimal code of conduct that directs how employees are treated with regards to wages, working hours, work conditions, safety signage and preventative measures such as lighting, electrical wiring and use of face masks, recruitment criteria, human resource policies in terms of disputes and promotions. What is absolutely essential is that they adhere to a set code of ethics to meet the compliance requirements.

Environmental compliance speaks to the respect that they have for environmental aspects such as the use of chemicals that may harm employees, disposal of waste products, pollution of water sources and the utilisation of environmental enhancing components such as the use of organic cottons. Compliance audits ensure that they meet the minimum standards of various environmental laws.

Capabilities refers to the standards of vendors and their sources such as mills, trimming manufacturers, distributors and other collaborators in the supply chain who are audited and assessed. They need to provide vital management control for process safety, security and risk management. Audits focus on the policies and procedures to verify compliance with regulatory requirements and industry standards. The programmes must be properly designed and implemented as well as identify deficiencies and recommendations can be made as to where corrective actions may be required.

Audits are done by stages, the first being the gathering of information through visual observation, documented reviews and interviews with staff. This data is then compared to the regulatory requirements and an evaluation is made as to how they conform to the legal stipulations which forms part of the pre audit. The second phase of the audit would be an intense on-site inspection which includes the conducting of interviews and review of records to assess the effectiveness of the implementation of programmes. Lastly the post audit consists of the briefing of management on the findings and the preparation of a final report and the relevant rating with corrective action recommendations.

Such audits should be conducted on an annual basis by a recognized audit company such as SMETA, WRAP or SA 8000. This should be followed up by physical visits to the plants. Audits are not limited to the point of manufacture but ought to also include the raw material sources, processing houses or any other out sourced functions at other vendors.

It is important that such reports are kept on record and up to date as in the event of a disaster such as a fire, building collapse or accident they will serve as critical points of reference.

Supplier introduction

Prior to commencing business with a new supplier it is required that the retailer briefs the supplier on all aspects of conducting business with them. This will apply to all processes that are in place to get them up and running and what is needed to be adhered to in order to maintain healthy relations thereafter.

The type of information that should be provided to the supplier is the background of the retail company and the philosophies as well as the type of operations in place so that they have a high level understanding of the company values that are subscribed to.

The supplier needs to have a crystal clear understanding of the end to end process which must be followed to become a certified supplier. This process will include the complete account registration, bank details and references, contractual agreements, settlement of payment terms and conditions and subscription to any software programmes that may be required to conduct business.

All conditions and guidelines in doing business should be outlined in a manual so that there is a detailed point of reference in the event of any dispute that may arise. Often the manual and other relevant information is available on the retailer's website for easy reference as is any training material together with ongoing updates and communications. The site may be access controlled even to the point that the information available is specific to the supplier. An example of such information is where the supplier is able to monitor the sales performance of their product in real time. It is essential that the channels of communication are structured and very clear as poor exchange of information has a negative impact and causes additional cost through wasted time, effort and resources which could result in late deliveries which will undoubtedly reflect in the end as lost sales.

Processes should be outlined for support and training usually in the form of instruction guides or is done practically in a lecture room environment. Representative topics would be for example, best practices for picking and packing, processing of orders and reporting availability of product. More technical training could be the procedures for the use of specific software packages, analysis and use of management reports or the use of a product critical management tool.

Performance management reports of the supplier should also be available in order that any shortcomings may be addressed promptly and enable the supplier to improve the efficiency of their operation. The type of key performance indicators that are measured, reported on and tolerances set are the analysis of customer returns, the measurement of actual variances to ordered quantities, the accuracy of picking and packing of product as well as the lead times of deliveries between receipt of orders and delivery to the retailer's receiving point.

A vital point to be measured is the rate of attrition during the production process which is the loss of product through rejects, under production through short delivery of raw materials or pilferage in the factory which results in loss of sales and needs to be analysed to keep these pre delivery instances to a minimum.

Customer returns must not only be quantified but the nature of the complaints have to be categorised and thresholds set to determine when a bulk return to supplier is warranted. The real danger lies where it is essential to retain the brand integrity when the nature of the defect can be considered dangerous or maybe life threatening and requires urgent withdrawal of the product from all points in the supply chain as well as the need to communicate a recall of the affected product through the media.

Where tolerances are set and the agreed criteria are not met, a consequence of some form or other may well be applied which usually has a financial implication through penalty discounts being enforced, rejection of delivery and the implementation of sale or return agreements.

Supplier manuals

The topics and information which is usually covered in the manual that may well form part of the memorandum of agreement between the retailer and the supplier are as follows

- The process that has to be followed to set up an account and the registration of the administrative details such as contact details, payment terms and logistical addresses. Retailer contact and help desk information is also published.
- Where the retailer may have unique software programmes for the conducting business such as the processing of orders, reporting of stock availability, the transfer of delivery instructions and product critical path management may require the

supplier to invest in the packages and if need be upgrade the hardware to meet specifications to run such packages.

- All details of systems and reports generated should be described in sufficient detail to allow the supplier to be able to refer to in order to resolve any queries they may have.
- Some retailers have an internet based portal system which may be accessed by all accredited suppliers each with their unique login where they will be able to view vital information, notifications, performance reports training documentation and operational manuals be able to order SKU tickets, view and download delivery instructions and any other critical information required to efficiently conduct business with the retailer

A typical greeting page after completing the login process would typically look like the illustration below

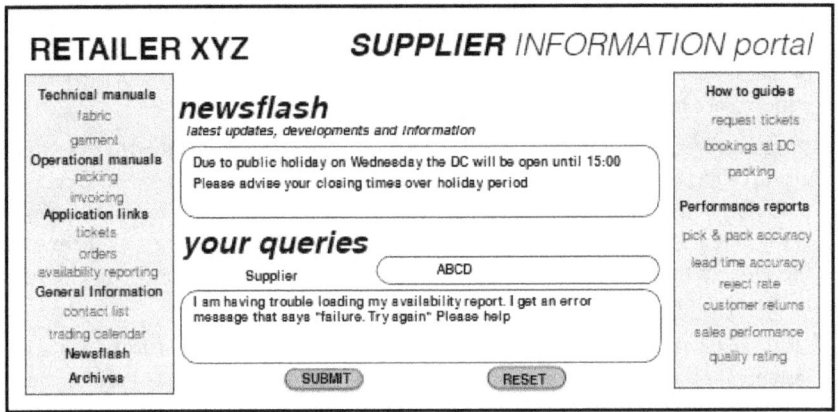

- The manual must outline technical guidelines and testing requirements as well as packaging specifications and approved suppliers should be listed.
- Invoicing methods and the information that needs to be appear on such documents as well as the payment channels and methods have to be described in detail.
- Ticketing details, ticket examples, reference numbers and order process should appear together with a list of approved ticket printing houses as well as the consequences which are in place should goods be delivered without or with incorrect ticketing.
- Packaging specifications should be itemised with regard to outer cartons, pack quantities, sealing guidelines, weight tolerances and markings which have to appear on the cartons.
- The guidelines and processes that need to be followed to complete the delivery of product to the retailer's receiving point in terms of equipment handling, time slot booking, descriptive labelling and the like must be described in detail.

- The shipping documents utilised and the information that is required for off shore need to be noted as well as any specific administration processes that have to be followed.
- A detailed description is included of performance indicators and tolerances that are measured.
- The penalty levels which are applied where performance criteria are not met should be clearly stated in the manual as well as the methodology of the calculation to avoid disputes if and when the occasion arises.

After the decision to consider an agreement with a supplier the retailer's technical team or an approved representative will visit the plant and perform an audit to ensure that the retailer's set down specifications and requirements are adequately met in terms of social, environmental and quality standards in order to be registered as an approved supplier.

If the supplier successfully meets the requirements a process will follow where the account is setup which will include the allocation of a supplier code which makes for easy identification on packaging and garment labels as well as administration of orders, deliveries supplier performance management.

Typical contractual contraventions are where the supplier's quality is found to be substandard and to be eligible for penalisation. Examples are quality failures in production, in cases where the safety of the product is compromised in the form of needle points or staples being found in the product, the use of poor attachments which carry the danger creating sharp edges on the garment that may pose a hazard to the consumer and the subcontracting of production to unauthorised vendors.

Clear guidelines and procedures as to the disposal of product need to be stated in the instances of the total withdrawal of product, production overruns, rejects and after what time period and which labelling or ticketing must be removed. Options that exist will be agreed on by the two parties for settlement of claims, for example, it may not be viable to incur reverse logistical costs to return distressed goods back to offshore suppliers and would be better to dispose of them locally. The recovery value would then be part of the settlement agreement with the supplier.

Protection of the retailer's intellectual property must be made very clear to all suppliers and this will pertain in the main to the safety of patents such as those relating to invention, utility or design. Trademarks are unique names, phrases, logos, symbols and can include colours which appear on the products themselves that are undoubtedly associated with the brand.

In the same way that the focus of the manual is on how to do things, the other side of the coin which is as important is the procedures to follow in order to exit from a supplier for whatever reason. It is not simply a case of no longer issuing orders and ceasing contact as there are certain processes which need to be clearly followed and signed off. These will include the deregistration of the account, the removal from all communication channels such as email distribution lists, elimination from access to any sensitive information on company websites and formal notification to all interested parties such as logistics, technology, marketing and financial departments.

The manual at times forms part of the memorandum of agreement between the retailer and the supplier and it is therefore extremely important that the contents are well understood by both parties.

Style briefing

Successful retailing is largely dependent on clear, accurate communication between the retailer and the supplier and therefore it is crucial that innovation and design takes place as quickly as possible in order that the completed product reaches the market place as quickly as possible. It is no longer just good enough to simply knock off samples from other markets or competitors as the modern consumer through the easy access to the latest trends via the internet are now much more knowledgeable in terms of what is the latest looks and are therefore much more demanding in identifying their wants in order to be as fashion relevant as possible.

Initially the supplier will be briefed conceptually what the product entails. The key information that is communicated is typically a sketch, photo, CAD print or sample with details. The detail will indicate design features, entail fabric and finish qualities, measurement guidelines, size range and ratios, colour ways, pricing and number of deliveries.

It is important that the supplier is provided with as much information as possible that is easily understood by even the most junior staff of the supplier especially in cases where English is not the first language. A principle of over communication and simplification should be followed to ensure complete clarity.

Meetings need to be handled professionally and follow a well prepared agenda and response to any queries have to be concise, well communicated and understanding needs to be tested. Detailed minutes and action plans with time scales attached should be clearly documented. Apart from the formal meetings, ongoing communications can be conducted via Skype and e-mail threads or conference calls.

Other information that can be included on a product specification document apart from the general information above is that pertaining to the inner packing, inserts and labelling. The product packaging minimum requirements and the methodology of the packing must be of a quality to withstand the rigours of transport, varying temperatures, inter warehouse transporting and mechanical handling.

A simple example of a style briefing sheet would look as follows

STYLE BRIEF		DATE	1 March
DEPARTMENT	Ladies T-Shirts	SUPPLIER	ABC
REFERENCE NUMBER	12345678	MNFR NUMBER	44455
DESCRIPTION	Ladies T-Shirt	SILHOUETTE	Top
DELIVERY DATE	20 September	NECKLINE	Round
UNITS	1,000	SLEEVE	Short
SIZES	Small 20% Medium 50% Large 30%	FIT	Regular
COLOURS	White 40% Beige 30% Red 30%	PRICE	129.00
FABRIC / YARN	100% Cotton Single Jersey Quality 12345	PHOTO / SKETCH	
STYLE COMMENTS	Piping must be contrast white.		

Specification pack

The product specification pack is the detailed briefing document managed by the buyer to clearly communicate the product details to the buying, design and technical teams as well as suppliers. The pack serves as a standardised way of clearly capturing all the information associated with a particular product. This is done at the highest level of detail which the supplier will need to achieve in order to meet the requirements

Components of the product specification pack

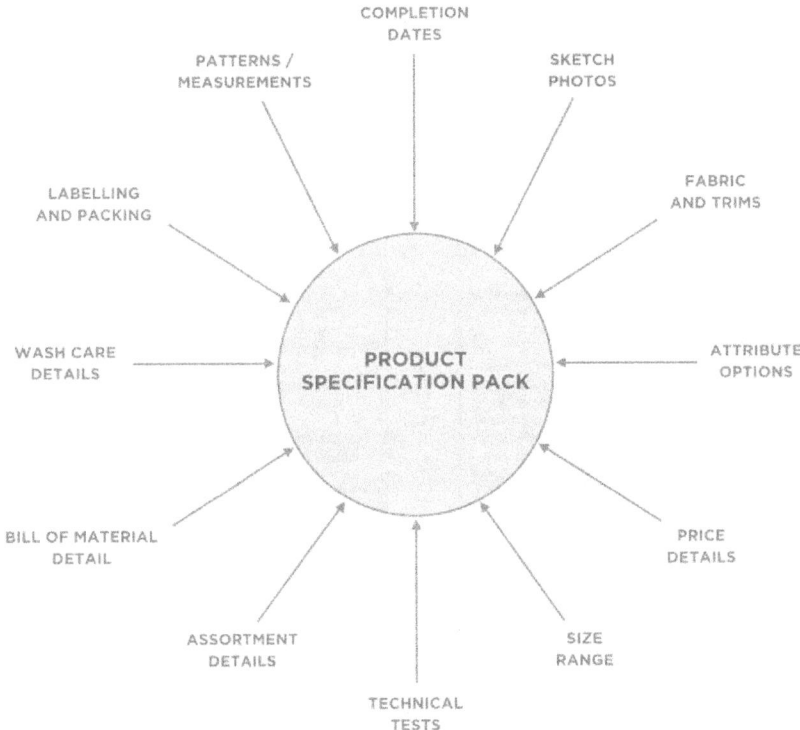

The type of information that should be included is

A sketch or digital picture, the season, the product name and reference number, fabric technical information, fit specifications, size details, quantities, sample sizes, delivery dates, packaging and placement of ticketing, outer packaging requirements, display materials such as hanger reference number, folding guidelines, details of required stitches and seams, trim card and placement details, garment sewing instructions, etc.,

This will enable the supplier to produce a first sample and provide a detailed quote of cost price. The. The technologist will be responsible to provide the bill of materials, the test requirements for the fabric, trim and product, any finishes that are required, safety requirements, fit and block stipulations, wash care instructions as well as provide an assessment together with the sourcing team of the supplier capabilities to produce the product.

The roles and responsibilities of the key buying team members can be depicted as follows

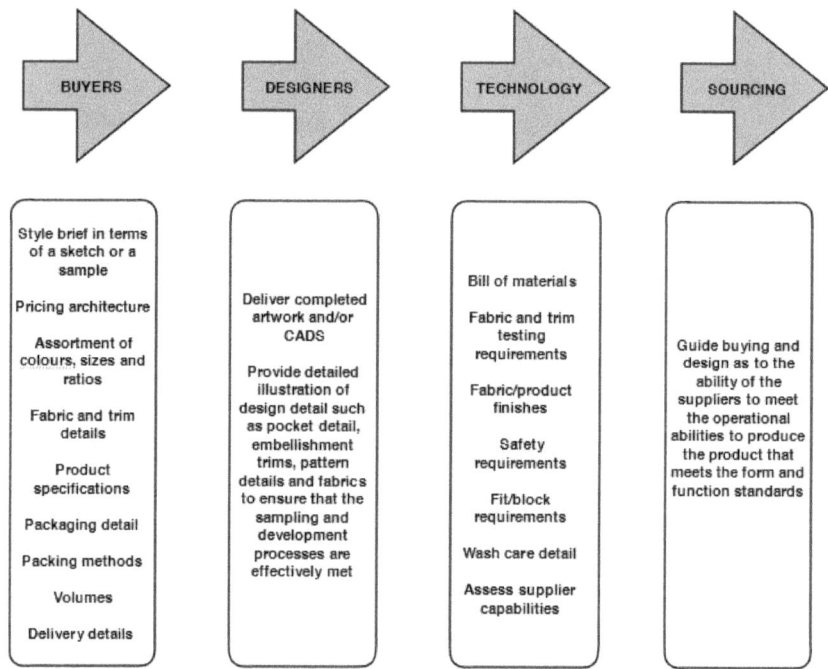

Supplier meetings

Once the product specification pack is formulated for a particular style, the retailer is in a position to initiate detailed meetings in order to prepare the supplier prior to the commencement of the production process.

During the meeting the specification pack will be discussed in detail with specific reference to the style as referenced on the style sheet, any print details or embellishments such as embroidery, accessories and trim details.

Any queries the supplier may have regarding fabric programmes, the logistical aspects, packaging need to be clarified and resolved.

It is extremely important that the meetings are well structured, prepared with an agenda, are clear and professional. Most importantly it is critical that the appropriate people are assigned tasks and completion dates are recorded for follow up.

Live information capture using a laptop and projector is very effective as meetings tend to be shorter, decisions and assignments are clear and results can be managed and tracked. The other advantage is that the publication of the minutes is immediate with the action tasks for those accountable being explicitly defined with completion dates.

It is also important to conduct meetings courteously, respectfully and where applicable be mindful of the culture of the supplier or vendor.

Negotiating

Negotiation is the process whereby through dialogue between two or more parties an agreement is met and the outcome satisfies the needs of both within the boundaries that the situation will allow.

In the retail environment, negotiations typically revolve around topics such as price, garment content, costs, innovation and profitability. The discussions can take place under high pressure where the expectations of both parties are elevated and the rivalry is intense. Often the relationship may be under threat which may or may not add another dimension depending how significant the association is. The opposite of this can be, and the most suitable, where the two parties collaborate to reach the most desired outcome.

To achieve a situation where both parties benefit, requires maturity, a clear understanding of the end objectives with informed discussions by both parties and the development of a plan to achieve a mutual objective.

Notwithstanding the above the supplier and the retailer will still have their own agendas. The supplier will wish to sell as much as he can for the best price while the retailer will want the product for as cheap as possible for the best quality. If the retailer does not have an insightful understanding of the manufacturing process the chances are that they might end up paying too much or sacrificing content.

Negotiating can be a traumatic experience and not all may have the appetite for the heightened discussion. In the case of the supplier there could be a tendency to avoid the confrontation and at times simply give the product to the retailer for the price requested, while the retailer, on the other hand, will similarly pay the supplier's more expensive proposal without exploring all options to get the best deal.

The retailer must always be well prepared with all relevant facts regarding fabric, trim, ratings and costs, prevailing exchange rate trends, wage structures, margin policies including other external and internal factors at hand in order to be able to have an informed sincere discussion. The persuasion process must be done in a way that the argument is convincing and the acceptance by the other party is seen to be mutually beneficial, trustworthy and incorporates the other participant's needs.

The progression of negotiation follows the steps of preparation, conducting the discussion and reviewing the outcomes.

Thorough preparation is critical which requires that the issues and opportunities are identified, prioritised and have a value for both parties. Focus must be on both the hard subjects such as the monetary issues and volumes as well as the softer matters such as perceptions.

Boundaries must be set in the types of outcome broken up into which would ideally like to be achieved, or what is likely to be achieved and thirdly the bare minimum that would be accepted.

Analysis of the environment of both businesses must be well defined in terms of the markets, competitor activities and the supplier capability and technical expertise required. These factors coupled to the trading history and what percentage the supplier is of the retailer's business and what the retailer represents of the supplier's total production or put differently, who needs who the most.

Past performance and consistency as well as the growth potential and the degree of product uniqueness or cost advantages are important leverage factors that are to be taken into consideration.

Key bargaining points for the retailer are cost prices, discounts, volumes, exclusivity, return policies, promotional support, delivery scheduling and any other unique service while the supplier's focus is likely to be the volumes that can be achieved, the highest cost price that will be agreed and the long term sustainability of regular business.

There is not always a satisfactory resolution to negotiation discussions and contingency plans need to be in place as to what alternatives are available should a deadlock situation be reached. These may include the possibility of moving production to different suppliers, reduce volumes and increasing the levels of other substitution ranges, the consideration of sale or return agreements and although not desirable, possibly increasing the selling price above the norm.

Behaviour and strategies during the meeting are extremely important. Asking for more than is expected will give room for negotiation to what is acceptable without simply accepting the first offer. It is also essential to remain flexible and creative in an effort to avoid a deadlock situation. A vital point to bear in mind is that at all costs to avoid haggling as this practice runs the risk of destroying a relationship.

If confrontation does transpire, it should be tactically done and at all costs does not include any personal attack or involve the use of threats and ultimatums. The power of silence should be remembered as it can be effective and if needs be, try and concede to small bits at a time, park potentially unresolvable issues even if it means that the meeting has to be temporarily adjourned.

There are personal factors that can influence the final negotiation. Different partakers follow different processes, they have diverse experience levels as well as possess varying understandings and personality traits which may be unpredictable.

There is an added complexity in dealing with off shore suppliers where there are duties, logistical challenges, and culture and language differences.

Once the negotiations are concluded, a documented summary of the agreements, commitment of resources, capacity to deliver and action plans is absolutely critical to ensure complete understanding. The record will enable an amicable resolution should any misinterpretation which could possibly become a point of dispute at a later stage.

Costings

It goes without saying that cost forms an integral part of the negotiation process. It is therefore imperative that the retailer has a good understanding of the components and the proportions of a costing sheet thus permitting the ability to test the validity and understanding of any costing presented by a supplier.

The cost of a product is broken down into two distinct categories, namely direct product costs and the costs associated in getting the completed product to the retailer.

Factors that will influence the cost of a product will be the size ratio, which if weighted towards the larger sizes will utilise more fabric or affect the wastage of fabric because of a less efficient marking of the lay of fabric on the cutting table.

The level of detail of the styling may not only affect fabric consumption, it will probably also influence the manufacture time or minute rating.

The width of the fabric can also affect the usage of fabric and the general rule is that the narrower the width of fabric the more expensive the product is likely to be. Specialist fabrics tend to be on narrow width such as 110cm while the full width is 148cm. Woven fabrics can be as wide as 160cm.

Plain or printed fabrics will also affect fabric usage particularly where stripes need to be matched on different components such as sleeve and body and is likely to result in more wastage of fabric.

The components of the cost of the products can be divided into those that are considered to be fixed such as raw materials, overheads which include services such as design, technology and logistics and those that are variable which are in the main the constituents that are squeezed down to meet the demands of the retailer like wages, working hours and production methods.

Packaging costs will also vary for different types of product. The size of the cartons required to transport the product is determined by the dimensions of height and width that must protect and accommodate the garment comfortably. The in store presentation requirements will also affect the overall cost from the point of view that allowance may be needed for hangers as well as additional swing tickets.

Where goods are imported, duties need to be taken into consideration. Duties are normally determined against the free on board value or in other words the cost to place it on the deck of the ship. They can also be calculated as ex works which is the cost as at the completion of production.

Exchange rates are a critical factor. The option to purchase currency ahead of time at a fixed rate to finance the cost provides the peace of mind that the costs will be stable even if the day to day rates fluctuate. If currency is not bought ahead but goods are purchased at the prevailing rates the retailer may be forced to revise selling prices to ensure the achievement of the target margin.

Different categories of products attract different tariff duties at the receiving country depending on country of origin and manufacture as well as protection policies of local production.

The cost to transport the goods from the place of manufacture will vary for local goods or from the port by the clearing agent, depending on the location of the retailer in relation to the supplier or port, the size of the cartons or container and the mode of transport. Included in this section would be freight and warehousing charges.

The typical elements of a product costing and examples of approximate proportions will be

ELEMENT	DEPENDENCY	CATEGORY
TRANSPORT 5%	Different methods of transport used.	Transport / landing 20%
DUTY 30 - 40%	Taxes levied against the import of goods as specified by the local government.	
SUPPLIER MARGIN 10%	Supplier margin can vary between 5% and 15%.	
WASH AND TRIMS 5%	Costs allocated to special processes or trims.	
PACKAGING 7%	Total cost of all packaging, including presentation.	Production costs 80%
LABOUR 28%	The standard minute rates will differ from country to country, depending on operational complexity.	
FABRIC AND MATERIAL 50%	Will be influenced by the garment rating, which will dictate how much fabric is used to manufacture the garment.	

In addition to the product costs as outlined above there are other costs that need to be taken into account in order to get product to market. These can be categorised basically into two categories, firstly being additional costs to the supplier such as the base overhead costs being the total for rent, electricity, administration costs and the like that will always be there and which must be apportioned per product unit.

The second category can be described as being unrelated to the product directly that have to be paid. The main type of such costs are settlement discount agreements, marketing contributions, finance costs and royalties. These together with the product costs will deliver the final cost of the garment.

Points to note in the review of costs are in cases where the supplier throws in vague and unsubstantiated reasons to justify increases. It is essential that the retailer tests such requests to ensure they carry merit.

A typical instance is where the statement is made that wages have gone up and a new costing is proposed. A cross check is required to determine the proportion of what labour represents of the total costing. In the above example this would be the 28% for labour and apply the increase to this part and reconcile to the proposal.

Where increases are attributed to material increases an effort should be made to investigate the trend in the industry and do some comparisons even if they may be a bit crude. If your research shows that the increase is not in line with the trend, the supplier should be encouraged to find a better source and not to pass on the cost of their inefficiencies.

The use of exchange rate fluctuations to motivate cost price changes is more easily resolved as the average movement can be tracked over a period of time and applied. It is a possibility that in fact there might have been an improvement. Foreign currency could also have an influence depending at what price the supplier or retailer may have covered forward.

If the retailer's volumes are increasing significantly the opportunity exists to negotiate a discount in cost price to share the benefits of the improved scale of efficiencies. A point to note is that while this practice is not discouraged, the smaller retailer may not be able to finance the larger volumes of product or growth based incentives. Even with the benefit of a greater margin, the viability remains to be dependent on the organic growth of the chain, for example, the addition of new stores in order to accommodate the higher buying volumes.

A costing approach which is often employed by retailers is that of requesting appropriate suppliers to tender for a product. In order that this is done fairly and equitably the exact same specifications need to be provided to the potential suppliers. Cross costing comparison between suppliers is a popular option where there are large programmes up for grabs and is unlikely to be used for once off high fashion inputs.

For a retailer to commit to high volume programmes, it is a key requisite that the potential suppliers fulfil some basic requirements in that they must be financially stable, have a reliable track record in terms of delivery performance, provide consistent quality with up to date compliancy audits and will be able to cope with the required volumes which could include the agreement to hold a minimum stock holding. The supplier should also be flexible enough to be able to make styling changes to the product where necessary.

The key stipulations for use with cross costing or tenders which will be provided is a detailed style sheet, comprehensive specifications of fabric and trims, the garment measurements with the range of sizes, volumes, a target cost price, packaging requirements and packing methods, delivery dates or production flow.

ORDERING

After the negotiations are completed and the decision to award the production of a style to the supplier is taken, an order has to be drafted to reflect the commitment to the supplier.

The signed order for the supplier is created and placed by the retailer for the entire season in the case of a continuity product or possibly monthly for input styles. It is imperative that it must be done timeously to ensure the required completion date is realistically achievable and the production lead time required will be determined by careful critical path production management.

While the order is in essence a contractual document it will be subject to the overall terms and conditions that are entered into in a memorandum of agreement that is drawn up separately when a manufacturer is appointed as a certified supplier. Production can only commence once the final approved order is in the possession of the supplier.

The contract or the order is the document that details the terms by which the retailer takes ownership of the goods in exchange or payment of an agreed price.

The timing of orders is done according to the range plan guidelines and each supplier will be provided with an extract specific to them for the season. This production programme will indicate the style details, quantities, size ratios and colour specifications which will enable them to plan the production capacity and will be used as the point of reference during follow up production progress meetings. Each style will also have a corresponding style specification sheet which confirm the costs, pack quantities, labels and tickets, wash and care details, testing requirements and the fabric as well as component information.

Orders may be amended where required. These adjustments are normally for quantities, dates, prices and size ratios. The changes need to be recorded on the contract and refer to the date of the alteration as well as the nature of the change.

It is advisable that any style changes require the order to be cancelled and be replaced by a new order as in essence it is a different product.

The order can have two status phases where a pre-production contract enables the supplier to procure fabrics, components, labelling and packaging and make a pre-production or pre shipment sample which will be submitted to the retailer for approval. The sample will serve as the set standard of quality that will be referred to should any disputes evolve in production or in stores.

Production may only commence once a final approved order is received by the supplier.

Documented programmes of continuity lines for the full season may serve as an authorised arrangement from which the supplier will be able to order the raw materials and components but they will only be able to commence production of agreed quantities, for example, for six weekly time periods upon the receipt of an approved contract. This gives the retailer the flexibility to make adjustments based on current performance. Such amendments may take the form of changes to quantities, size ratios and colour quantities.

Dependent on whether the supplier is local or offshore the delivery requirements need to be clearly outlined with all relevant contact details, delivery stipulations, carton markings and delivery addresses.

In the case of a local supplier, delivery is normally to a designated warehouse at an approved time. Off shore suppliers may have to deliver to an offshore centralised consolidation centre where the goods will be amalgamated by shipping agents into containers prior to shipping.

Payment will be made in the foreign currency and will be dictated by the international commercial (INCO) terms applied.

Common INCO terms for the payment of imported goods will be FOB (Sea Freight) which is where payment is prior to shipment by sea either by bank wire or a letter of credit. The purchaser's bank releases payment upon receipt of certain documentation such as the bill of lading, packing lists or commercial invoice and is due when the goods are loaded on the ship and ownership is then transferred to the retailer. If the INCO term is FCA it carries the same conditions as FOB except that the transportation is by air.

CFR (Sea and Air Freight) describes the situation where the supplier is responsible for the costs of transport to the destination port. While ownership only transfers when the goods reach the destination, the retailer is responsible for the goods while they are in transit and therefore they would have to take out insurance for this period. If the supplier does this then the INCO term applied is CIF (cost, insurance, freight).

Added to the costs are government duties which can be applied in the form of a percentage dependent on the various customs categories that the product falls into.

In terms of air freight it should be noted that the cost is often prohibitive as it is dictated by volume and weight and therefore is usually only applied to small and high value items or where an urgent stock need is required in order to meet a launch date.

When placing orders for imports it is critical to take into account the lead times that need to be added on to ensure the required delivery and launch dates are met. Lead time can be described loosely as the time that it takes for product to be delivered from the factory to the back door of the retailer's warehouse or distribution centre. This becomes increasingly complex when the factory is off shore as there are a whole host of additional activities that have to take place before the retailer eventually receives the goods.

Pre shipment activities may involve the delivery to an off shore consolidation centre where different orders may be combined to make the full use of a container cost effective. Part deliveries in different containers can also make the consolidation and sequence of packing more complicated where there are different orders possibly also for different retailers.

In terms of the pre shipment critical path that needs to be adhered to prior to shipment is triggered by the supplier's confirmation that this will be met about three weeks before the ship date and approximately a week later the forwarder will advise the vessel and booking details at which time the supplier will send the pre shipment sample to the retailer with quality audit reports to request approval to ship.

A typical order for imported and local products will probably be as follows

ORDER										
RETAILER XYZ										

ORDER NO		DATE	
SUPPLIER		ORDER STATUS	Pre production / Production
SUPPLIER REFERENCE		COMPLETE/SHIP DATE	
PAYMENT TERMS		LAUNCH DATE	
DELIVERY METHOD		PACK QUANTITY	
DELIVER TO		TOTAL QUANTITY	
		COST VALUE	
		SELLING VALUE	

SKU NUMBER	STYLE NUMBER	STYLE DESCRIPTION	COLOUR	TOTAL COLOUR UNITS	SIZE	TOTAL SIZE UNITS	COST PRICE	SELLING PRICE
100023564	12345	Basic t-shirt	White	1000	S	200	45.00	99.99
100023565					M	400	45.00	99.99
100023566					L	300	50.00	110.00
100023567					XL	100	50.00	110.00
100023568	12345	Basic t-shirt	Black	2000	S	400	45.00	99.99
100023569					M	800	45.00	99.99
100023570					L	600	50.00	110.00
100023571					XL	200	50.00	110.00

BUYER SIGN		MANAGEMENT SIGN			
MERCHANDISER SIGN		SUPPLIER SIGN		DATE	

The information typically included on the order is as follows and will be stored on a data base system for any interested party that needs to access the detail.

Supplier reference number and name

Order number

Date that order was raised

Port of loading

Shipment date and launch dates

Shipping method

Method of payment

Payment terms

Point of delivery

Style number

Style description

Colour break down and quantity

Labelling instructions

Special terms or conditions of trade

SKU number

Size breakdown

Quantities

Cost Price less any negotiated discounts

Selling Price

Number of cartons

Carton dimensions

Number of units per inner pack

Number of inner packs per outer carton

Signatures of authorization to buy are most commonly those of the buyer, merchandiser and a member of senior management. The omission of any of the signatures could result in the order being rendered invalid in the case of a disagreement. A supplier signature is often the rule but the acceptance of the order is in essence the recognition of all the terms and conditions of the order.

It is not uncommon for planning production schedules or provisional orders to be handed over to the supplier prior to the issuing of an official order, particularly in the case of replenishment product where the supplier needs to plan capacity requirements, order raw materials and components but this is by no means the go ahead to commence production. Without the completed signed order no knife may be put to the fabric.

The higher level order may be supplemented by a detailed specification pack and a critical path management document that serves as an appendage to the order and reflect the details and quality references of the fabric and components, sample submission requirements, technical tests, labelling instructions, packaging reference numbers and specifications.

The buying and merchandising team will use the basic information to interrogate orders at any time to check, monitor and if required will amend the orders which may be, for example, quantity or date related. Other areas of operation or parties will also need to have access to orders in order that their activities are completed timeously to safeguard that the final completion date is met.

Technology has to utilise the detail to ensure in the process of managing the critical path that all tests, quality control during the manufacturing process, garment fittings and rail samples are completed timeously.

The finance department need to know all the costing details and terms of payment as well as the proposed selling price to ensure that there is sufficient cash flow available to enable payment and be able to monitor the achievement of the gross profit margins.

The IT departments need to be aware of all orders for the provision of the SKU numbers as well as cater for the generation of the swing tickets or labels that are attached to the garments indicating the style number, colour, size and price detail which are either sent to the suppliers in bulk or the data files are transmitted to those suppliers that have the facilities to generate their own SKU tickets.

The distribution centre must have sight of the orders in the pipeline to assess the size of proposed deliveries going forward to ensure that they are in a position to plan sufficient resources in terms of staffing, equipment, space capacity and that sufficient transport is booked to deliver the goods speedily to stores.

The space capacity requirements both in the warehouse and stores will depend largely on the packing configurations in terms of the storage outer carton which is how the goods will be stored, allocated and transported to stores and the inner packs which are otherwise known as the saleable unit that will be presented to the potential consumer.

Examples of packing configuration below where selling units of t-shirts is singles and are packed ten in an outer carton and where socks selling units is in a three pack and there are ten three packs in the outer carton

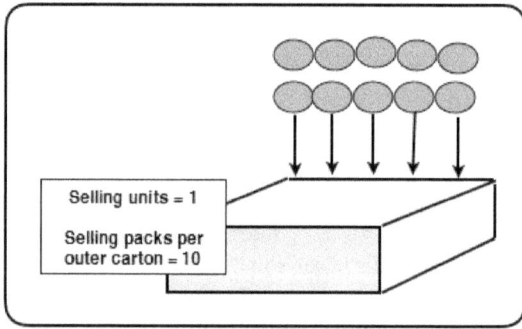

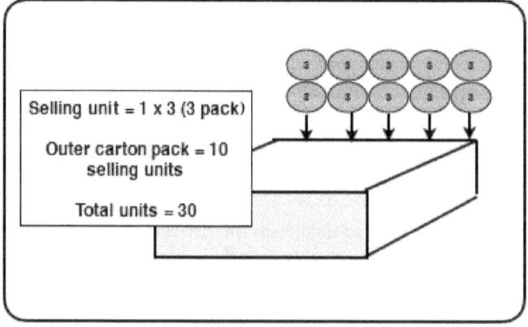

CRITICAL PATH MANAGEMENT

Critical path management is undoubtedly one of the key philosophies that needs to be applied in production management in order to have control and knowledge of the work flow in the production of garments. This achieved by the setting up of a timeline that reflects the anticipated critical deadlines that have to be achieved in order to meet the required delivery date of the order and being completely aware of the impact of late deliveries of fabric and components on the realisation of this objective. Without the knowledge of all statuses the consequence could well be the late deliveries with the application of penalties or even worse the cancellation of orders.

Through the management the entire flow of product workflow through the view of progress from concept to completion allows the effective planning of tasks and reallocation of resources to minimises bottlenecks, identify due dates and milestones as well as highlight areas where attention is required. And thereby keep suppliers on schedule as well as encourages collaboration between the different teams. A major benefit is that critical path management allows management to move away from day to day reactive management into a more strategic management role aligned with strategic business objectives.

Ideally a critical path management tool should possess characteristics such as flexibility that enables the tool to be configured to meet the customised requirements of the user. Alerts should be built in to notify stakeholders directly through SMS, emails or pings and Information should be able to be automatically rolled up with an analytical ability to be able to drill down to prescribed levels or issues.

The interface ought to be user friendly and easy to learn, easy to update and where web based tools exist they should be compatible and easily accessible within a range of internet speeds, browsers and levels of internet sophistication that allows global interaction with suppliers in order to track the progress of the product from the sampling stage through to delivery. As supply chains grow in complexity with increased production volumes and links in the supply chain information visibility is imperative in order to facilitate complete transparency while also highlighting the ramifications of poor decision making and poor capacity management.

Some of the software tools that are available in the market place which assist in the monitoring of production progress and are accessible to all stakeholders do come at a cost and albeit expensive the benefits of the investment may well be justified.

Alternatively if the product is too expensive it is well worth developing one's own instrument even though the tool may well be cumbersome and more complex to apply but at least it will provide rough idea of the lead times required for the procurement of fabrics and components for the completion of orders and therefore In order to guarantee the on time launch of the product and the management of the path of product development. Without this the retailer ends up flying blind and often only finds out about delays from the supplier close to the expected delivery date when it is invariably too late to take corrective action. It is not uncommon to hear of the cancellation of large volume contracts worth great values as a result of the relatively low cost care labels not being available on time and thus the completion of the delivery date is compromised. It is not only the physical components that can cause issues the added value outsourced services such as embroideries, pattern making or packaging can in the same manner impact the delivery status if they are not completed on time.

Unfortunately with multiple versions of documents such as cost sheets, design samples and supplier scorecards in differing formats which provide an inadequate platform to share information can result in a lack of awareness into potential supply chain problems and an inability to provide early warnings and synchronise real time responsiveness.

All stakeholders involved in the process, which includes the buyers, suppliers, product technologists, fabric technologists and commercial management need to focus on the critical path management of the product.

The key stages or milestones which are in the main controlled by the buyers and technologists that need to be scrutinised are the style briefing and finalisation, colour approval, fit approval, bulk test of fabrics and components, approval of the pre-production sample, pre-production meetings with the supplier and final approval of the pre-shipment or rail sample prior to production at which point the product development can be considered complete and the launch date is able to be confirmed.

The monitoring of the process needs to documented and highlighted in some form in order that key players are able to measure the actual accomplishment of tasks compared to the required completion dates. If collaboration and communication is ineffective, bottlenecks are likely to occur, production and delivery deadlines may be missed, and penalties will be applied with the resultant squeezing of margins. The purpose of such reports is not only to ensure that the critical milestones are met on time but also serve as a reference for meetings to identify possible delays and decide what actions need to be taken to improve or correct the situation.

In principle the lead times are measured in weeks and the relevant dates are attached starting from launch date which represents zero days and progressively working backwards taking the time for the completion of each stage into account and ending up where the no later than date for the starting style brief stage is determined.

The format of the critical path action plan may well vary from retailer to retailer dependant on the level of detail the measurement takes place in terms of each operation.

The hierarchy of the reporting and performance measurement is usually done at style level and all the styles for a department can be rolled up to departmental level and then up to group level. These together with supplier extracts and other filters make for effective performance management of both the retail teams and the supplier.

An example of a basic critical path management tool which highlights the key milestones, time line and progress monitoring with analytical properties is illustrated below.

PRODUCT DEVELOPMENT MANAGEMENT							Style Brief		Style Finalised		Colour Approved		Fit Approved	
Supplier	Grp	Dept.	Style	Colour		Total	Complete	In-complete	Complete	In-complete	Complete	In-complete	Complete	In-complete
abcd	1	123	44445	Black	Units	1000	900	100	800	200	900	100	750	250
					%	100	90%	10%	80%	20%	90%	10%	75%	25%
					Weeks	39			29		24		11	
					Date	10-Oct			17-Dec		15-Jan		15-Apr	
Supplier	Grp	Dept.	Style	Colour		Total	Complete	In-complete	Complete	In-complete	Complete	In-complete	Complete	In-complete
abcd	1	123	55555	White	Units	1500	1300	200	1400	100	1450	50	1500	0
					%	100	87%	13%	93%	7%	97%	5%	100%	0%
					Weeks	39			28		24		11	
					Date	10-Oct			17-Dec		15-Jan		15-Apr	
Supplier	Grp	Dept.	Style	Colour		Total	Complete	In-complete	Complete	In-complete	Complete	In-complete	Complete	In-complete
bcde	2	124	55556	Yellow	Units	2000	1500	500	1400	600	1600	400	1800	200
					%	100	75%	25%	70%	30%	80%	20%	90%	10%
					Weeks	39			28		24		11	
					Date	10-Nov			17-Jan		15-Feb		15-May	
Supplier	Grp	Dept.	Style	Colour		Total	Complete	In-complete	Complete	In-complete	Complete	In-complete	Complete	In-complete
cdef	3	128	44445	Green	Units	1000	700	500	900	100	800	200	750	250
					%	100	70%	30%	90%	10%	80%	20%	75%	25%
					Weeks	39			28		24		11	
					Date	10-Dec			17-Feb		15-Mar		15-Jun	

PRODUCT DEVELOPMENT MANAGEMENT							Pre-production sample & supplier meeting		Pre-shipment sample		Launch Date	
Supplier	Grp	Dept.	Style	Colour		Total	Complete	In-complete	Complete	In-complete	Complete	In-complete
abcd	1	123	44445	Black	Units	1000	750	250	750	250	750	250
					%	100	75%	25%	75%	25%	75%	25%
					Weeks	39	8		2		0	
					Date	10-Oct	06-May		17-Jun		01-Jul	
Supplier	Grp	Dept.	Style	Colour		Total	Complete	In-complete	Complete	In-complete	Complete	In-complete
abcd	1	123	55555	White	Units	1500	1500	0	1450	50	1500	0
					%	100	100%	0%	97%	3%	100%	0%
					Weeks	39	8		2		0	
					Date	10-Oct	06-May		17-Jun		01-Jul	
Supplier	Grp	Dept.	Style	Colour		Total	Complete	In-complete	Complete	In-complete	Complete	In-complete
bcde	2	124	55556	Yellow	Units	2000	1800	200	1700	300	1900	100
					%	100	90%	10%	85%	15%	95%	5%
					Weeks	39	8		2		0	
					Date	10-Nov	06-Jun		17-Jul		01-Aug	
Supplier	Grp	Dept.	Style	Colour		Total	Complete	In-complete	Complete	In-complete	Complete	In-complete
cdef	3	128	44445	Green	Units	1000	850	150	950	50	950	50
					%	100	85%	15%	95%	5%	95%	5%
					Weeks	39	8		2		0	
					Date	10-Dec	06-Jul		17-Aug		01-Sep	

QUALITY MANAGEMENT

Quality is defined as the combination of design and properties that are required at an acceptable level to perform the ideal form and function requisite to serve the market for which it is intended. In the textile and apparel industry the quality is calculated in terms of quality and standard of fibres, yarns, fabric construction, colour fastness and the final finished product.

Quality control starts with ensuring that the fabric being utilised meets the required specifications to be transformed into a perfect garment and therefore needs to be managed and inspected for faults which are marked. The length and width of fabric have to be checked to ensure that they meet the specified measurements and thereby do not affect the cutting table lay. It is important that the fabric is inspected upon receipt and meets the finished width and stability while the garment must be sound with regards to seam construction and the stitch forming action.

The supplier will need to have the fabric and trims tested by a recognised laboratory to record that they meet the weight, width and yarn specifications. Tests also need to focus on the performance of fabrics such as rub tests or how the fabric reacts in a washing machine in terms of colour fastness and shrinkage.

In the manufacture of garments the objective is to achieve the right final product on time. The final product specifications are dependent on the level of the quality control present in sampling and development departments that from samples to completed production, including layout and process stipulations, the construction parameters and measurement of performance. In order that this done effectively robust recording systems should be in place as well as checklists for the supervisors to logically ensure that all critical points are covered and are within the set down tolerance levels are measured as per performance analysis and reporting. Reporting will outline results of quality control during garment assembly, number of marks and stains on garments, analysis of the cost of faults and directives as how to improve garment cleanliness.

It is vital that proper quality control is applied in order that the product presents well on the shop floor, fits well, wears well, washes well, is functional and represents value for money to avoid the loss of sales through customer returns or the depletion of units during production which results in under deliveries and ultimately lost sales. The points of quality control are conducted throughout the supply chain process which includes those prior to production, during in line production, at dispatch stage and on the shop sales floor.

A quality controller needs to possess certain abilities that will equip them to ensure that a thorough and complete monitor is done. The key attribute required is that of the need to pay attention to detail along with assertiveness and transparency. Tasks have to be conducted professionally and ethically. The incumbent must be prepared to be open minded and consider alternative points of view. The nature of the job requires tact and diplomacy and in certain situations the quality controller is required to be culturally sensitive. Decisiveness together with collaboration is paramount to ensure that quality standards are maximised.

The various steps of quality control and types of checks in the manufacturing process is illustrated below

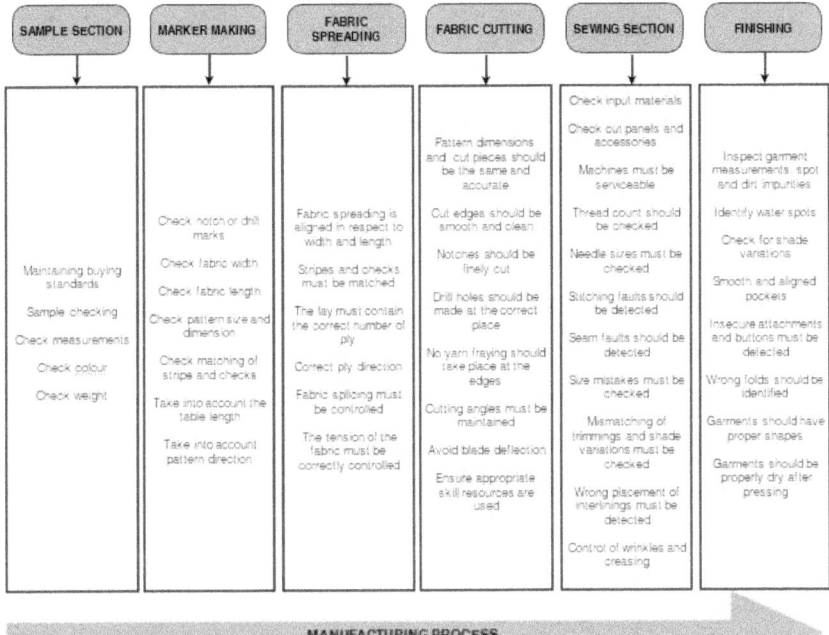

SAMPLE SECTION	MARKER MAKING	FABRIC SPREADING	FABRIC CUTTING	SEWING SECTION	FINISHING
Maintaining buying standards	Check notch or drill marks	Fabric spreading is aligned in respect to width and length	Pattern dimensions and cut pieces should be the same and accurate	Check input materials	Inspect garment measurements, spot and dirt impurities
Sample checking	Check fabric width	Stripes and checks must be matched	Cut edges should be smooth and clean	Check cut panels and accessories	Identify water spots
Check measurements	Check fabric length	The lay must contain the correct number of ply	Notches should be finely cut	Machines must be serviceable	Check for shade variations
Check colour	Check pattern size and dimension	Correct ply direction	Drill holes should be made at the correct place	Thread count should be checked	Smooth and aligned pockets
Check weight	Check matching of stripe and checks	Fabric splicing must be controlled	No yarn fraying should take place at the edges	Needle sizes must be checked	Insecure attachments and buttons must be detected
	Take into account the table length	The tension of the fabric must be correctly controlled	Cutting angles must be maintained	Stitching faults should be detected	Wrong folds should be identified
	Take into account pattern direction		Avoid blade deflection	Seam faults should be detected	Garments should have proper shapes
			Ensure appropriate skill resources are used	Size mistakes must be checked	Garments should be properly dry after pressing
				Mismatching of trimmings and shade variations must be checked	
				Wrong placement of interlinings must be detected	
				Control of wrinkles and creasing	

MANUFACTURING PROCESS

The purpose of the pre-production meeting conducted for every style is to set the standards to which the quality will be measured during production.

The pre-production sample serves as the basis of discussion and all key stakeholders will be present from both the retailer and the supplier. Technology representatives and the buying team must attend together with supplier teams to determine the criteria for sewing, finishing, fabric, trim, quality assurance, cutting, production and packaging management. At these meetings the technical requirements are stipulated and agreed for the make-up, sewing and thread combinations, the special methods that are needed to handle trims in bulk production, the wash and product finishing standards as well as the packaging and shipment methods. Any special processes out of the ordinary must be well documented and the minutes of the meeting must be recorded and signed off by all participants to ensure there are clear reference standards in the event of any difference that may transpire at a later stage.

If required it may be decided to produce wearer trials to assess the performance of the product in relation to the technological test standards especially where physical or chemical laboratory tests are not appropriate or it is not able to be spot checked in bulk production. All in all the purpose of the pre-production meeting is to identify risk areas which may result in product failure or possible injury to the customer and establish preventative measures.

During production the quality audits must include the assessment of care labels, packaging, price tags, colour and the quality of garment finishing and conformance to measurement specifications. The main visual checks will include the button attachments, non-inclusions of seams, fabric flaws, elastic failures, colour mismatches, poor make up and appearance, sew ability of threads have to be checked to ensure there are no broken threads, evidence of skipped stitches and that the stitch spacing is balanced. Safety issues such as needle points or staples in the product are also watched out for.

Final inspection will include will focus on ensuring the consistent colour shading of all parts of the garment, that the garment is balanced in terms of collar, pockets and cuff attachments as well as the critical measurements and weight are within the acceptable tolerances and that all accessories are securely applied and are functional.

It is important that the audit report is completed speedily in order that preventative measures can be documented and action plans are implemented. The number of garments that must be measured and assessed is determined by agreeing the sample survey percentage that will represent the total quantity and what tolerances are allowed before rejection takes place.

The amount to be inspected may vary from no inspection to 100% inspection and may or may not include random inspections. Statistical sampling may be determined that would represent the amount that could be extrapolated to be the character of the total quantity.

It is assumed that 5000 pieces are purchased with the breakdown and sample survey quantities as follows

	WHITE	BLACK
SIZE M	1 500	1 200
SIZE L	1 500	800

Of the 5 000 units, it is agreed to check 30% visually and measure 10%

VISUALLY INSPECTED	WHITE	BLACK
SIZE M	450	360
SIZE L	450	240

MEASURED	WHITE	BLACK
SIZE M	150	120
SIZE L	150	80

Graphically the inspection sample can be depicted as follows

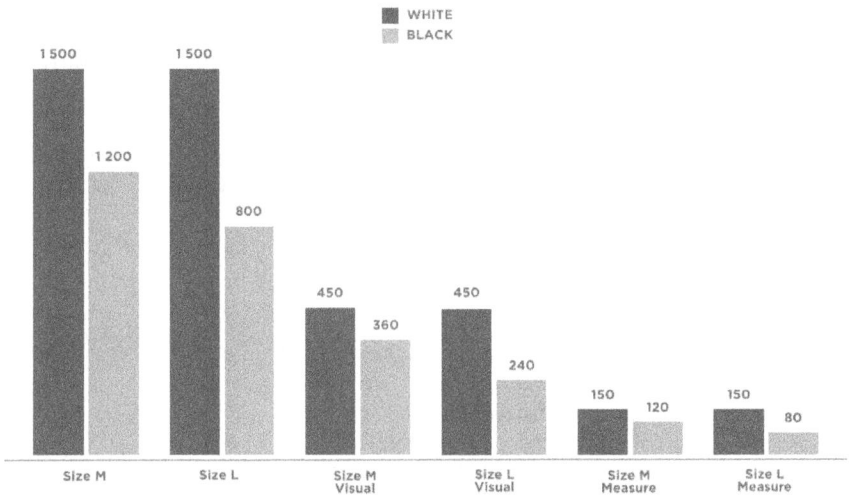

A typical measurement sheet will look like the example below

QUALITY MEASUREMENT AUDIT REPORT												
DEPARTMENT	**XYZ**	**STYLE**	**STYLE DESCRIPTION**									
COLOUR	**WHITE**	**SIZE**	**SMALL**			**MEDIUM**			**LARGE**			
OP NO	**DESCRIPTION**		**SPEC (cm)**	**1**	**2**	**3**	**SPEC (cm)**	**1**	**2**	**3**	**SPEC (cm)**	**1**	**2**	**3**
1	Across front		35				37.5				40			
2	1/2 chest		48				53				56			
3	1/2 hem		46				51				53			
4	Shoulder		13.5				14				16			
5	Overarm sleeve		18				21				23			
6	Underarm sleeve		7.5				9				11			
7	Across back		38				40				43			
8	Neck drop front		8.2				9.5				11			
9	Neck width		18.2				19				21			
10	Neck drop back		1.5				2				2.5			
INSPECTED BY			**TOTAL MEASURED**				**COMMENTS**					
			RESULTS									
SUPPLIER			Out of tolerance									
			In tolerance									

In addition to the production line audits it is also necessary to conduct quality inspection in stores which apart from identifying and resolving quality issues there is the added advantage of interacting with sales teams and share knowledge and learnings from those at the coal face who interact with the customer.

Apart from the skill levels and components which may affect the quality of a garment there are other factors which need to be taken into account. For Chinese suppliers it is important to consider production which takes place close to the Chinese New Year holidays. Not only is it the completion of orders prior to the commencement of holidays which could put pressure on the rate of production the other real risk is the start-up time taken by factories after the holidays. This is often a slow process due to the fact that many of the workers who travel inland to their villages are tardy in returning back to work or take extended leave which results in broken production and the use of lower skill levels to complete more complex operations. This phenomenon is part and parcel of doing business with Chinese suppliers and contingencies need to be put in place as invariably suppliers who do not have the capacity to complete orders on time which were optimistically accepted as well as the fact that raw material suppliers experience the same phenomenon also puts excessive strain on the production lines to meet deadlines timeously. In summary careful planning with built in safety stocks to ensure continuity of supply to the stores is paramount.

Environmental circumstances such as storms which prevent ships docking or deviate from their routes, power failures, strikes, goods being held up at customs or other unforeseen events can delay the arrival of raw materials and finished product and may impact eventually on the timing, quality and quantity being delivered.

SUPPLIER PERFORMANCE MANAGEMENT

In order that supplier performance will be at consistently high standards there must be a solid foundation of core requirements in order to achieve the objective at hand. While it is important that performance is influenced external environmental factors and the customers that are served the most influential factor that impacts the operational efficiencies is undoubtedly the management of the organisation.

While the day to day measures are important, some of which may be minor such as containing canteen costs, time keeping, rental and logistical costs and the like it is critical that management focus on the longer term issues such as staff training and development, process control, maintenance, production planning and the consistent achievement of set down performance indicators.

Such a set of performance indicators are cascaded down through the organisation and as a result each employee is constantly aware of how they are being evaluated and whether they are adequately meeting the standards for which they are held accountable. The pay structure, including bonus incentives should be in place based on the achievement of the recognised KPI's.

It is equally important that management maintain their visibility on the production floor and interact at all levels in order to keep motivation at high levels with good communication and also when they relate to retail customers they are able to do so with knowledge of the hands on challenges.

Safety has to be promoted to the fullest with respected and assertive safety teams in place that have the support of senior management, and all staff should be equipped with appropriate effective personal equipment.

Research and development departments should continually be innovating, testing and improving products while apart from a robust preventative maintenance programme the reinvestment in the company by the owners is key to maintaining regular customers and attracting new ones.

The objective of achieving zero defects and delivering optimum quality is done through the building and sustaining of relationships by continually assessing, anticipating and fulfilling stated and implied needs.

It is important that service level agreements are set up front and are understood and committed to by all. SLA's clearly define the clients can expect from service providers and outline what their responsibilities are. This ensures protection for both parties and promotes beneficial long term relationships.

The risks that can be encountered are aggravated in certain situations such as with the movement of strategic product to new plants, or existing suppliers being utilised for different types of products which they may not adapt well to. The allocation of high volumes with a minimal quality assurance infrastructure in place as well the ability to meet critical launch dates require that performance measurement is critical for early identification of any potential failure.

A tough line has to be taken on dealing with substandard delivery and quality. Data collected from various sources needs to be accurate and reliable especially where a penalty system is applied for non-performance.

Customer returns have to be analysed and criteria put in place which may result in a penalty being applied for the number of returns in the form of a sliding scale. The analysis of the most common faults also highlights the areas of quality which need to be addressed.

The late or under completion of orders or non-conformance to size and colour ratios translate directly to lost sales and can be assessed and penalized either through a direct fine or a trade discount and possibly a sale or return arrangement. A word of caution with regard to a sale or return arrangement is although the goods that are not sold after a period of time can be returned, the sales of these goods may impact the performance of other similar products that are on offer at the same time which is not always taken into account.

Late deliveries measurement ensures that completion is on time according to the critical path. A typical example of a penalty is one which is on a sliding percentage scale of discount for every week that the delivery date is missed up to a pre-determined stage after which the order faces cancellation.

Lead times can be measured based on the time taken for the supplier to deliver to the retailer's back door. A realistic number of days can be set as a tolerance for the delivery of product based on mode of transport and distance from the retailer thereafter penalties may be activated. It does happen that the supplier may report the full availability of product but in reality part of the order may still be in production and the delivery may take place in the form of a number of split drops which would be unacceptable and is almost equivalent to fraud.

Order fill percentage represents what was actually delivered in comparison to what was ordered. Any deviation to this translates into lost sales from the lowest size level as the retailer is not receiving what was ordered.

Ticketing must be accurate as an incorrect ticket which is scanned in will be captured erroneously on the stock data base and sales at the till point will be incorrect thus distorting the product's data integrity which will only be rectified once a physical product count is completed. Sample checks upon receipt of product will help identify such errors and enforce the implementation of a penalty system. Often the attachment of incorrect SKU tickets could be as a result of poor communication and disciplines between the retailer and supplier, poor control at suppliers or non-destruction of old SKU tickets at times of a price changeover.

The advantage of a controlled performance management system is the quick identification of poor performing suppliers. The more efficient suppliers welcome the performance measurements as it assists supplier management to more effectively manage their business, assign accountability and also be able to assess their contribution to sales performance and strive to benefit from the advantage of incentive schemes applied by the retailer where they exist.

It is not surprising that the garment manufacturers are in turn also applying penalty systems and clauses in the contracts with their raw material suppliers such as the fabric mills and trimmings suppliers.

It is preferable that a reporting system is entrenched and is published on a monthly basis to the supplier and the internal buying groups. Such reports form a good basis of discussion in meetings with the supplier and alerts the buying team to potential problems that may be evolving. It should therefore be no surprise to the supplier if the need to apply penalties is necessary as sometimes the monetary value of the penalties could pose a major financial risk to a supplier.

Supplier meetings where qualitative feedback and their performance measures are discussed encourages commitment between the two parties and promotes collaboration. At such meetings the sales performance of the products specific to the supplier is analysed and understood. This may lead to the formulation of action plans where required and may include cooperation and coordination of marketing activities which could comprise of cooperative advertising and media campaigns. Part of the discussion would include the sharing of information regarding consumer, product, market trends and new innovations.

It is as important that the retailer probes the supplier's expectations in the relationship with the various operational and management structures of the retailer. This can be conveniently done through a scheduled survey, possibly annually or seasonally, an example of which is outlined below.

Buying

- Is it easy to communicate with the buying team?
- Are you clear in terms of what they expect from you with regard to costs and deadlines?

- Are the general terms and conditions understood?
- Do you have any suggestions to improve the relationship?

Quality and compliance

- Do you receive clear guidelines and know what standards need to be followed?
- Do you receive sufficient feedback?
- Are approvals of samples received timeously?
- Do you have any suggestions to improve the relationship?

Product development

- Do you receive clear briefing and information about new products
- Do we take into account the configuration and specifications of your production processes?
- Do you have any suggestions for improvement?

Relationships

- Is there sufficient interaction with higher levels of management
- Do teams visit frequently enough?
- When teams visit you, do they behave in a professional manner?

Our service providers

- Are the courier services meeting expected standards?
- How efficient are our freight forwarders?
- Is our QC audit firms applying similar standards as ourselves?

CONCLUSION

Partnerships between the retailer and the supplier is an essential pre-requisite to ensure the success of the retailer. There has to be a circle of trust to promote collaboration and mutual respect. As has been highlighted the only guarantee about change is that there will be change and it is without doubt that the retailers' greatest ally when change happens, whether it be positive or negative, is their source of supply. The support of the supplier through their flexibility and ability to appreciate the need for revolution is vital for the shared destiny and the celebration of success for both businesses through maintaining healthy relationships with the customer. From get go there has to be a circle of trust to promote collaboration and mutual respect.

The seamless integration of roles and activities of all stakeholders is essential to ensure that the end objective of servicing the customer with the highest quality product that is fully functional which effectively meets the consumer's aspirations and expectations in terms of style, price and consistent availability.